*WHY?*BUT I HAVE TO

ALICIA MOORE

S.H.E. PUBLISHING, LLC

Why? But I Have To

For information contact :

SHE PUBLISHING LLC | Munster, IN & Indianapolis, IN

Email: info@shepublishingllc.com
Website: www.shepublishingllc.com

Tel: 219.515.8032

ISBN: 978-1-964061-28-3 (paperback)

Cover and Title Page Design by Michelle Phillips of CHELLD3 | 3D VISUALIZATION AND DESIGN

First Edition: March 2025

10 9 8 7 6 5 4 3 2 1

Table of Contents

Dedication

I dedicate this book, *Why? But I Have To*, to our Lord and Savior, Jesus Christ, who has been so faithful in my life.

Acknowledgments

I would like to express my deepest appreciation to all my family and friends that believed in me and my weight loss journey.

Chapter One:

380

Life can be very interesting. Before you know it, you may not even realize who you've become. I was 380 pounds.

Yes, I really didn't know who I was. The only thing I knew was that I had experienced a lot of trauma in my life, starting with a miscarriage in early 2005, followed by the death of my father and a bad breakup. I was simply just living life.

I was so proud of closing on my first home in August of 2006, and when I looked up, I was 380 pounds. I didn't realize how much weight I had gained, and my blood pressure was out of control. I knew I had to do something.

I worked so hard day and night, just thinking about providing a home for my son and starting fresh—not really focusing on my health.

But if you don't have your health, you really don't have wealth.

1st Healthy Tip:
Drink Alkaline Water

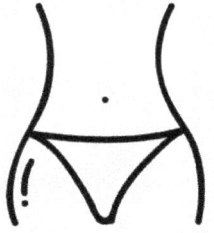

Benefit:

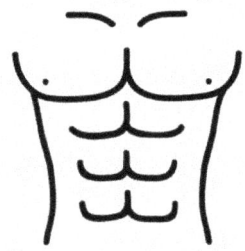

Alkaline water, also referred to as ionized water, has a pH level greater than 7. The main reason people choose to drink alkaline water is that it helps balance the pH levels in the body.

A person with a high level of acidity in their body may drink alkaline water to balance out these levels. Increasing the alkaline levels in the body will neutralize the acid. Consult your doctor, but it is generally recommended to drink about three or four glasses of alkaline water each day to help level things out in the body.

I completely get it—being 380 pounds didn't happen overnight. Years of trauma in my life, breaking up with my fiancé, sitting at my desk for 10 to 12 hours per day working, and eating pretty much whatever I wanted (which was a lot of bread, rice, and potatoes) contributed to my unhealthy habits.

I didn't feel my best. Not only did I have high blood pressure, but I also developed acid reflux (GERD), which stands for gastroesophageal reflux disease.

This digestive disease occurs when stomach acid or bile flows into the food pipe and irritates the lining. Acid reflux and heartburn more than twice a week may indicate GERD.

I went to the doctor, and I was told that I needed to lose weight or risk developing esophageal cancer.

GASTROESOPHAGEAL REFLUX DISEASE

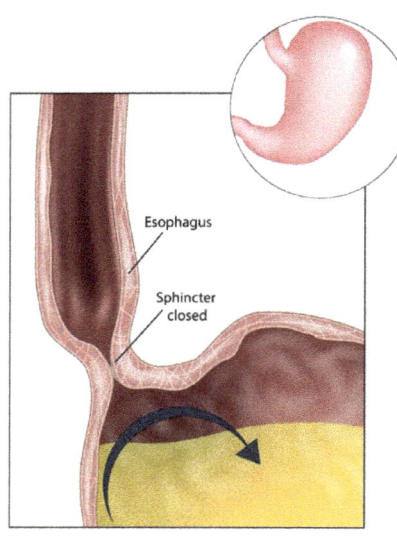

Esophagus

Sphincter closed

Healthy stomach

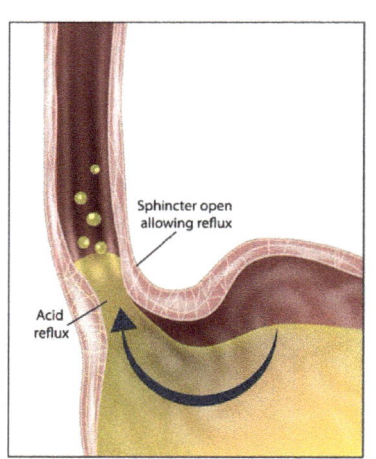

Sphincter open allowing reflux

Acid reflux

Gerd stomach

Scripture for Strength

Psalm 59:9, 16, and 17

"You are my strength, I watch for you; you, God, are my fortress, my God on whom I can rely... I will sing of your strength; in the morning I will sing of your love; for you are my fortress, my refuge in times of trouble."

2nd Healthy Tip:
Meal Prep

Benefits of Meal Prep:

- Can help save money
- Can help save time
- Can help with weight control, as you decide the ingredients and portions served
- Can contribute to an overall more nutritionally balanced diet
- Can reduce stress as you avoid last-minute decisions about what to eat or rushed preparation

Chapter Two:

2016

August 10, 2016, started out really great. I had just come back from a fun outdoor vacation, and I had a blast, but my body was telling me something different. I didn't feel well and was experiencing a lot of low back pain, which normally doesn't last for hours. I felt off, so I decided to go to urgent care to get checked out. When I arrived, I simply stated that my lower back was hurting.

The nurse began taking my vitals, measuring the body's most basic functions. She looked closely and asked if I was feeling dizzy. I said no. Then she advised me that I was at heart attack and stroke levels—my systolic pressure was higher than 180, and my diastolic pressure was over 110. I didn't think much of it. She asked if I was taking any medication, and I told her I had stopped taking my meds because I thought I could control my blood pressure on my own. I didn't like the way they made me feel—sleepy and tired all the time.

At that point, I knew it was time for a change. I agreed to receive care and immediately started blood pressure meds through an IV because the nurse felt that if I refused care, I would risk having a heart attack or stroke. Thank you, nurse, you saved my life. Please, get checked regularly—it's so important.

August 10, 2016, was also my grandfather's birthday. He passed away due to high blood pressure and had a heart attack. I am so grateful to be here to share my story.

All I could think about was seeing my son grow up. He was a teenager, and I knew I wanted to live. I simply started taking my meds. I wasn't very happy about it, and falling asleep at my desk from time to time was not what I had imagined my life would be like. This can't be how it ends.

I knew I needed to do more, so I started by going to the gym and getting on track with exercising. But it wasn't enough—I really wasn't losing weight and was maintaining my weight at 319 pounds.

I went for my annual checkup and started talking to a nurse about my weight. I knew I needed to do more, so she suggested I start a new weight loss program. I agreed.

October 28, 2016, was the day my whole life changed for the better—It was a Friday. I talked about all my bad habits and daily routines.

I must admit, the first 30 days were tough. I had to learn how to eat all over again. I started journaling my food and stepped outside my comfort zone, letting go of old bad habits.

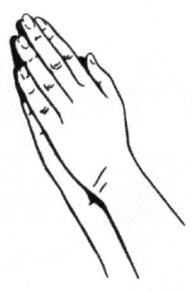

Philippians 4:13

I can do all things through Christ who strengthens me.

My eating habits started to change as I tried and tasted different, healthier food options. I wasn't sure if I was going to lose the weight, but I knew nothing beats a failure but a try. Wow—no bread, rice, or potatoes? That's what I liked to eat!

If I was going to succeed, I knew my lifestyle was a personal and conscious decision to perform behaviors that might either increase or decrease the risk of disease. You've got this!

Chapter Three:
Lifestyle Change

2 Corinthians 12:9: "My grace is all you need, for my power is the greatest when you are weak."

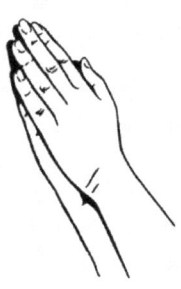

Fitness is the result of proper nutrition and conditioning. It is a state of physical and mental well-being. Health, on the other hand, is a much broader term and varies from individual to individual.

I really just wanted to maintain my health and help others achieve the goal of becoming healthy, so I decided to focus on improving myself and building my strength. I worked out at many gyms, including swimming, spin classes, and cardio, which were never difficult for me. However, I did notice a change in my strength. I started surrounding myself with people who shared the same lifestyle goals as me, and I also became more involved in outdoor activities.

I began working out with Coach Byrd, the owner of Byrd Chest Fitness. I was actually very nervous at first. I had to learn how to use my body; I had always relied more on machines, so it was difficult for me initially. But with God's strength, I was able to trust my body, and it felt great. This allowed me to help others along the journey as well.

In March of 2020, everything started shutting down due to the pandemic, and I wondered where and how I would continue working out. Coach Byrd simply stated, "We are going to work outside." I thought, "Okay," and it turned out to be exactly what I needed. It kept me mentally and physically strong, and it allowed me to continue helping others. We even traveled to several states to host boot camps.

Thank you, Coach Byrd, for not only allowing me to be a part of Byrd Chest Fitness but also for giving me the opportunity to become an indoor cycling instructor.

Take care of your body, and it will take care of you. Drinking plenty of water, eating fruit, fresh veggies, and protein works wonders for the body. I feel wonderful knowing I've been given the chance to live a healthy lifestyle—thank you, God. We're not perfect, but I want you to know that change is possible. Don't get me wrong, I have bad days with my eating as well, but I know and realize that eating healthy not only makes me feel great but also helps me look great.

Healthy Tip:

Flush Out Inflammation

Vegetables: Broccoli, Kale, Brussels Sprouts, Cabbage, Cauliflower

High-Fat Fruits: Avocados, Olives

Healthy Fats: Olive Oil, Avocado Oil

Fruits: Blueberries, Pomegranates, Grapes, Cherries

Please, please, please write it down and make a food journal. Two shakes and a healthy meal were a good guide for me. Staying between 1200 to 1600 calories a day was a must. I never thought I would survive, but it worked. The one thing I suggest and know is to watch your food portions—yes, it matters. How much are you eating?

What's in your cart? A lifestyle change comes with a lot, so here's a quick guide for you: fresh vegetables, fruits, protein, snacks, hydration, and vitamins. Self-care is important too. If possible, find time for yourself because if you're not together, how can you help others? Some self-care ideas include a massage, pedicure, wellness retreat, or sitting by the ocean—those are my go-tos.

In Conclusion:

I know there are many things that need to be removed—sugar is a big one. For example, soda and juice. Start replacing those with healthy, lean meals and drink plenty of water.

Losing 200 pounds didn't come easy—I had to work hard for it. You can do it too. I'm here to tell you, look at me. I never in my life thought I would lose over 200 pounds. I simply wanted to be healthy and reduce my blood pressure. I also had GERD, which I've talked about before. It's a chronic disease where stomach acid or bile flows into the food pipe and irritates the lining. I maintain my progress because I know how I used to feel, and it wasn't good at all.

I definitely suggest staying active—we were meant to move, not sit. Stay committed; trust me, it's one of the best decisions I have ever made. You've got this! I love seeing people achieve their weight loss goals, and I love motivating others as well. Stay healthy—you only have one body. Well, I've had the opportunity to live in two different bodies. Thank you, God, for allowing me to help others.

I've struggled with my weight for years. Every day, I wake up praying for the opportunity to help someone with their weight loss journey, knowing that it's truly a gift from God. I overcame high blood pressure and acid reflux, and I knew I was at heart attack and stroke risk levels. That's terrifying. To have the opportunity to share my story and pray that this book reaches millions of people struggling with obesity is a blessing.

Stay committed. Drink plenty of water—sometimes we may feel hungry, but we're just actually dehydrated. Keep moving, stay active—you are amazing, and you can and will succeed. God sends people into your life for a reason. Along my journey, Coach Byrd has pushed me at times when I thought I couldn't go any further. He encouraged me to become a fitness instructor, and he helped me create a stable lifestyle. Change is possible.

Romans 15:13: "Now may the God of hope fill you with all joy and peace in believing, that you may abound in hope by the power of the Holy Spirit."

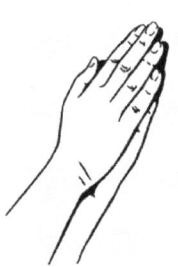

Chapter Four:
Childhood
Habits

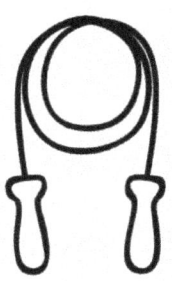

Growing up as a child was absolutely amazing—I couldn't have asked for a better childhood. Thinking back, my parents loved feeding me, but I also started developing some unhealthy habits. First off, I know what I really enjoyed: drinking Kool-Aid. However, what I was putting in it was a different story. Some of the things I added were very unhealthy. For example, I added a lot of sugar, and while it tasted great, I now know that a lot of sugar was not the best option. I also started drinking a lot of juices and soda, which also contained a lot of sugar. When I think about it, I actually had more sugar than water, but as a kid, I was simply enjoying my choice of beverages.

My daily eating habits weren't always the best. I also enjoyed a lot of junk food, like chips and candy. I wasn't really interested in food—just junk food—and going outside to play. I stayed active, but my food choices weren't healthy. I also ate breakfast, lunch, and dinner whenever I felt like it. During the week (Monday-Friday), and especially during summer break, breakfast usually consisted of cereal and milk. Yes, I had 2% milk with cereal, and sometimes two bowls. On weekends, particularly Saturdays, we would have breakfast as a family, which typically included rice, scrambled cheese eggs, bacon, and biscuits. It was delicious! On Sundays, I usually fasted or drank a glass of orange juice before church. After church, I would have dinner with my family, which often included mustard greens, cornbread, and short ribs—so tasty! For dessert, I would have pound cake or banana pudding. Shout out to my grandmothers, grandfathers, and parents for those delicious meals.

Before I knew it, I had developed a really bad habit of consuming sugar. Most of my snacks were cupcakes, Ding Dongs, and honey buns. They tasted good, but looking back, I know I should have been eating more veggies like carrots, broccoli, asparagus, kale, and spinach. It all starts with habits and what you're eating at home. I remember eating a combination of fried and baked foods. Some of our dinner choices included fried catfish, baked chicken, fried pork chops, fried chicken wings, hamburgers, and homemade French fries. I also developed a habit of eating hot foods and spices—hot chips, hot sauces—and while I had these habits, I was still active. I spent time outside, riding my bike, jumping double Dutch, and playing tag (or whatever we called it). I also played cards, like spades, outside with friends and went to the park a lot.

Growing up was sweet, but I was always chunky—I was never a small child. Family vacations were a blast! Every year, we would go to Mississippi and Wisconsin Dells. Both of my parents were from Mississippi, so we had a lot of family to visit. The cool thing was that we would always have huge gatherings like BBQs, and my dad would go down South to get our meat. We also had family reunions, usually around the 4th of July, with over 60 family members gathering in Mississippi at once. We had homemade cornbread, biscuits, sweet potato pie, homemade cornbread dressing, and potato salad. I know, a lot of carbs—but it was so tasty!

I always enjoyed seeing my family, and we had an amazing time. I thank God for my family and friends. However, there were also challenges, like not knowing when enough eating was enough. Over time, I began to gain weight because I didn't really watch my portions. It's important for kids to learn portion control. You can overdo it with portions, so be mindful! A cupped hand is equivalent to a ½-cup serving. You can use this tool to measure food items such as pasta, potatoes, nuts, and even ice cream. A cupped hand equals ½ cup, and the palm of your hand equals 3 oz. You can use your palm to estimate protein intake as well.

In conclusion, I had a combination of sweets and fried foods, but I also lacked knowledge about portion control and indulging in food and snacks. I really should have added more vegetables, alkaline water, and lean proteins into my daily routine. I was simply just being a kid, but it's important to work on our health. Health is wealth.

Chapter Five:
Corporate America

Life definitely changed for me when I became a full-time mom and worked full-time. That was my life for 18 years, and I definitely had my ups and downs. I was always busy, whether it was planning birthday parties for my son or finding fun events and hanging out with family and friends. Outside of work, cooking, and taking care of responsibilities, that was my life.

My eating habits didn't change much—I still enjoyed a lot of carbs, which I almost had every day. Some of my favorites were bagels, cornbread, and biscuits. I worked a lot of overtime, so I didn't have much time for meal preparation. My focus was mostly on Sunday dinners and a few other meals throughout the week, like tacos, pot roast with carrots and potatoes, and cornbread. I mostly ate out, often choosing fried, greasy foods. Working in corporate America, food was always available if you were meeting your numbers or attending special events. We had everything from pizza to fried chicken to subs.

I didn't do much working out because I was so focused on working and providing for my family. I just didn't make the time, but now I know that finding balance is key. I do realize that my portion sizes were out of control—I was overeating. I thought I was just living life, but looking back, I see the need to make healthier choices. I drank a lot of sugary beverages when I should have been drinking more water to stay hydrated and adding extra calories to my meals in the form of vegetables and fruit. I was so focused on carbs—bread, rice, potatoes—that I didn't even think about protein at the time.

I would sit at my desk for 10 hours or more each day, and I remember eating a lot on my days off, especially on Saturdays when I was out shopping, including grocery shopping for the week and household items. I became a young mom at 21, so I had a lot of responsibility, but I always stayed prayed up and kept going. I would get my annual check-ups, and the doctors would tell me to lose weight because my blood pressure was always on the borderline of being high. I'd lose 15 pounds but then gain 5 back. I always had a gym membership, but I'd take a lot of breaks. I wasn't consistent and didn't hold myself accountable.

Now, my diet has changed drastically. I include more green vegetables and fruit, fewer carbs, and sometimes no carbs at all. I eat off a saucer to watch my portion sizes, drink plenty of water, and have fewer sugary beverages.

Overall, you have to learn to make better choices because we only have one body to live in. In my case, I was given the opportunity by the grace of God to be in a healthier, happier body.

In conclusion, I want you to understand how important it is to keep moving and stay active. Life can be stressful, and it can feel difficult because we have so much to do—getting ready for work in the morning, fighting through traffic, or dealing with public transportation. There are so many things on our plates, and it can become overwhelming. But working out is definitely a plus. It helps relieve stress, manage weight, reduce the risk of disease, strengthen bones and muscles, and improve your ability to do everyday activities.

Chapter Six:
New Lifestyle

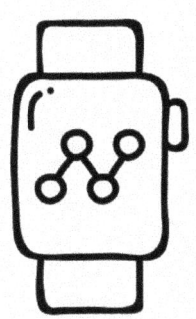

I finally decided to make a career change after 17 years. Corporate America just wasn't working for me anymore; it no longer interested me, and I knew I had a higher calling. I decided to go back to school for massage therapy in 2013 after a car accident. I didn't realize how much I had neglected stretching, had poor posture, and was constantly in pain, particularly in my shoulders and neck. I literally took pain meds to help me sleep at night. Never in a million years did I think it was because I wasn't staying hydrated, stretching, or exercising.

After physical therapy and chiropractic care, I felt amazing. I was so interested in the field because, if I felt this great, I could help others feel the same way—absolutely amazing. Simply staying hydrated, stretching more, and getting adequate rest can definitely improve your life. Not to mention, making healthier choices and staying active. There's so much more I can offer the world—a more glamorous life. I didn't realize that my life was about to change for the better.

I really enjoyed learning about the body. I was so nervous about becoming a massage therapist, though. I had never really interacted with people face-to-face; I was used to communicating over the phone. Asking questions and getting to the root cause of a problem face-to-face was more challenging than anything I had experienced before.

I'm currently a massage therapist, and it has been five years. I've learned so much about the body, making better food choices, and exercising. It's amazing how the body has the ability to heal itself. I help and educate individuals daily about staying hydrated, stretching, and getting the proper rest. Doing so will make your body feel so much better. Adding more green vegetables like kale, spinach, and broccoli, as well as fresh fruit, will not only make you feel better but will help you look amazing too.

In conclusion, I have so much more to share with you. Not only do I have more to discuss, but I'll also dive deeper into relationships, setbacks, and comebacks along the way. It's not easy, but it's worth it. Be on the lookout for my next book!

About the Author

Alicia K. Moore is an entrepreneur, massage therapist, body sculptor, weight loss motivator, and business-woman who has dedicated her life to helping others achieve their wellness goals. With a passion for empowering individuals to lead healthy and fulfilling lives, Alicia has made a significant impact in the field of health and fitness through her company, Moore Glamorous Life.

As the founder and CEO of Moore Glamorous Life, Alicia has created a platform that inspires and motivates people to prioritize their well-being. Her ultimate goal is to instill a sense of confidence and vitality in individuals, encouraging them to make positive changes in their lifestyles. By combining her expertise in massage therapy, body sculpting, and weight loss coaching, Alicia has become a prominent figure in the wellness industry.

One of Alicia's greatest achievements is her personal journey of transformation. She has successfully shed over 200 pounds, becoming an inspiration to countless individuals struggling with weight loss. Her experience has given her a unique understanding of the challenges and triumphs associated with making sustainable lifestyle changes.

With her infectious energy and unwavering determination, Alicia serves as a motivator and role model for those seeking to improve their health. She firmly believes in the power of hydration and encourages everyone to prioritize drinking plenty of water. As she says, "Hydration is the key to unlocking our full potential and maintaining a healthy body and mind."

Alicia's work extends beyond her entrepreneurial endeavors. She actively engages with her community, conducting workshops, seminars, and wellness retreats to spread her message of health and vitality. Her commitment to making a positive impact has earned her recognition and respect from both her peers and clients.

Through her holistic approach to wellness, Alicia K. Moore continues to empower individuals to take charge of their lives and make lasting changes. Her expertise as a massage therapist, body sculptor, weight loss motivator, and businesswoman, coupled with her personal transformation, has made her an influential figure in the wellness industry. Alicia strives to inspire others to embark on their own journey towards a healthier, happier, and more glamorous life.